Theories of Everything

Also Some Opinions & A Few Sketchy Facts

StoryPeople
Decorah

ISBN 978-1-937137-76-2
LCCN 2012947786
Copyright ©2012 by Brian Andreas

The people in this book, if at one time real, are now entirely fictitious, having been subjected to a combination of a selective memory and a fertile imagination. Any resemblance to real people, or real situations, you may know, is entirely coincidental, and is a reminder that while it may seem real, it's still only your personal theory. As the author is fond of saying, just because you think it, doesn't make it true.

All rights reserved. No part of this book may be reproduced or transmitted in any form or by any means, electronic or mechanical, including photocopying, recording, or by any information storage and retrieval system, without permission in writing from the Publisher.

StoryPeople
P.O. Box 7
Decorah, IA 52101
USA
563.382.8060
563.382.0263 FAX
800.476.7178

storypeople@storypeople.com
www.storypeople.com

First Edition: *October, 2012*

To my sons, Matthew & Gabriel, for hours of laughter & conversation & the endless theories we've shared. Zombie invasions. Chemtrails. The real purpose of life & a host of others I can't even begin to remember. I cannot imagine the world without you in it...

Other books by Brian Andreas available
from StoryPeople Press:

Mostly True
Still Mostly True
Going Somewhere Soon
Strange Dreams
Hearing Voices
Story People
Trusting Soul
Traveling Light
Some Kind of Ride
Peculiar Times (e-book)

Theories of Everything

Also Some Opinions & A Few Sketchy Facts

Introduction

One day, I was sitting at my drawing table, looking out at the bees in the garden & almost without thinking, I picked up my pen & started to write. Here's the story that showed up:

> Once upon a time there was a boy who knew what he was going to be from the very moment he was born. As soon as he was able to talk, he told everyone, I am a builder of dreams. No one in his family had any idea what that meant, except maybe his Aunt Dorothy, who knew about dreams & how they form you into the thing you're going to be, even when you think you have other plans.
>
> The rest of his family did things like work with numbers & fix old cars & bake bread in a bakery. When he first told them what he was going to be, they thought it was cute & then, when it didn't stop, it was something not to be mentioned at family gatherings & finally, it was something that would lead to personal suffering if he didn't start getting his head on straight, by god. So, he stopped saying it out loud, but he never forgot & when he got older, he moved away & his family told the neighbors he was working as a manager & everyone nodded & was pleased that he'd finally come around to viewing life as it was & not how you wish it would be.
>
> But he didn't really care because he was building things of air & sunlight & the laughter of children & the sharp smell of lighter fluid at a summer barbecue & the flash of color on the throat of a hummingbird & all of them were things that had no real name, but people felt them all the same. They felt them all the same...

That was my first clue that I was going to do another book.

My second clue was the next night, when the title came to me in a dream: Theories of Everything. There was something instantly satisfying about that. I think it's because that's what we humans do, we make up theories about everything. There's very little we really know, so we make it up & then believe it, until reality clearly tells us that our theories aren't working any more. Then we go & make up something new & start the whole game all over again.

One late night while I was working on this, a curious thing happened. All of the pieces that were going into the book, the serious, playful, loving & anxious pieces, were scattered in front of me on the table. I sat there, looking at them, wondering if I'd be able to make sense of it all & just like that, I knew. There was nothing missing. These stories & thoughts & drawings & my life were all the same. I make things up because I'm alive & I like to jump in with both feet & see what I think about things. There's no right theory & no right answer. There's only this moment, fresh & new & what we do with it.

There is no real name for that, though, perhaps, grace comes closest, but we feel it all the same. It's something I wish for each one of you, knowing that there's nothing missing, that we're perfectly at home in our lives any time we're ready to see it...

With love,

Brian Andreas

Victoria Garden Mews,
Santa Barbara, California
17 September 2012

How to Write Something True

1. Forget everything you know & everything you want to say.
2. Listen to the quiet voices of the world. Start with your heartbeat.
3. Touch the pen to the paper. Feel it, the way it is only at one point all the time. This is the place writing shows up.
4. Write one word at a time. This will take more effort than you think.
5. This kind of writing doesn't care what you know, because you already know it. This kind of writing just wants to see what happens next.
6. When you can do this easily, go back to #1 again. This time no pen, no paper.
7. Live. Now you have something true to write about.

Why do we believe stuff that's not true? he said & I said because it's easier than admitting we don't know. Which is a lot closer to reality.

Free Admission

It's not that I'm not serious, he said. I just don't think of it as a career like the rest of them.

Serious Decision

Do you know that 90% of your brain works without using any words at all? she said. Just so you know, that means there's only a 10% chance of me making any sense at all once I start talking.

Playing the Odds

Just so you're prepared, he said, I'm going to ask you a question & I'm expecting a useful answer.

I nodded & sat up in my chair.

Let's hope it's something I can lie convincingly about then, I said.

Best Shot

> things I end up saying because it gets too quiet in here & I can't stand it.

> things I have words for that I don't really believe

> things I'm feeling in my body that I don't have words for. Yet.

> things that are beyond words that when I say them they sound like echoes of important things, only far away & more like mumbling

> things I say without thinking. Sometimes I wonder who's actually doing the talking, but most people who hear them seem to think they make sense, even though there are times I wonder if they're just humoring me

> which can lead to paranoia really quickly. I try to keep this to a minimum

Using Words: A general diagram in case you've been having questions

Word Choice

It's not surrendering to the
Universe, he told me, if
all you're doing is sitting
around waiting for it to
turn out like you hope.

Partial Surrender

I had a lot
of dreams
last night
that meant
something,
but today I'm
back to my
waking life

& nothing makes
sense like usual.

Usual Sense

Most of the world's problems would disappear if we didn't have to be right. Unless you are.

In which case, everyone else just needs to listen better.

Listen Better

I'm not sure how to say this, he said, but you're wrong.

You're right, she said. You don't know how to say that.

Two Wrongs

deciding everything is
falling into place perfectly

as long as you don't
get too picky about
what you mean
by place.

or perfectly.

Falling Into Place

A Short Treatise on the Nature of Love

Point #1: I fell in love with my French teacher in the 7th grade.

Point #2: I have always loved languages & people who speak them.

Point #3: Even though my French teacher was married (how is that possible when we were both so young?) & she was (admittedly) older, we were about the same height, so I knew we could make it work, if she ever came to her senses.

Point #4: I no longer believe Point #3, for a number of reasons.

The Nature of Love

I don't know exactly what
she wants, he told me,
but I think I'm involved
   in some capacity

   whether I'm interested,
   or not.

   Into the Breach

I just want
to be loved,
she said

   & I said
   That's easy.

She stood there
for a moment &
then she sat down
right next to me.

   Well, she said,
   there are a few
   other things
   on my list, too.

   Short List

How long does it take
to love someone? he said
& she shrugged.

Usually not too long, she said.

It mainly depends on
how many times you've
done it badly before.

Track Record

I used to love the
quiet, he said,
but then I met
her & now
the quiet
can't wait
for her to
show up to
tell her how
the day went.

Quiet Self

I always thought there'd be enough
time for everything & just today I
figured out that's true as long as
I don't expect to be alive for it.

Time for Everything

I think I've fallen in love, he said, but I'm out of practice, so it could just be because she hasn't yelled at me like everyone else I know.

Out of Practice

I'm no more deluded than the next person, he told us once. I just don't care who knows it.

Public Access

I pray in a non-specific way, he said & I said, What's that look like?

& he shrugged & said, Usually it's 'Come on baby, Daddy needs a new pair of shoes.' Then he smiled wide as the sky.

I figure that's probably why my life is turning out this way, he said.

New Shoes

Need to Know

I want to be loved for who I am, she said, because being loved for who I'm not just stresses me out.

Love Match

You are a treasure beyond price, he said & she smiled & said you don't know me all that well & he said that's why he didn't make an offer over the phone & then he squeezed her & she couldn't help but laugh.

Priceless

I want a man exactly like you, she said, except he'd listen to me no matter what.

A man exactly like me, I said, would know better than that.

Close Match

I'm not judging you, she said. I'm judging me for putting up with you. Then she patted me on the arm.

Good talk, she said.

Self Critical

You are not easy to love, I said. Oh, I'm easy to love, she said, I'm just difficult to please.

Those are two entirely different things.

Easy to Love

Let's save time, I said, & you tell
me what you want.

Who cares about time? she said.
It's more fun if you start
guessing & I'll tell you
if you're close.

Guessing Games

In Relationship
Math I've found
that even when
I'm right some
of the time, the
times I'm wrong
outweigh those
about 10 million
to 1.

Basic Math

I'll give you almost all my heart,
she said, except for a small piece
in case things go bad

& she couldn't see why
he didn't jump at it.

Reserve Judgment

How do you find your path? she said
& I shrugged.

>Mine has a lot of chocolate on it,
>I said, otherwise, I'd be as lost
>as everyone else.

Clear Path

>I'm not sure what I think
>about him yet, she said,
>because so far I've only
>imagined him in my mind
>& he still listens to almost
>everything I say.

Perfect So Far

I love people, he said. They're like free entertainment if you don't let them get to you.

Love Fest

I just want a little man of my own, she said.

Only without all the quirky personality issues I'm going to have to train out of him anyway.

Little Man

You don't hear a thing I say, she said. That's not true, I said. Like that last thing? I heard it & I agree completely.

Selective Hearing

I like things to be clear, she said. At least from your side.

My side's going to stay fuzzy until I get my way, she added.

Clear Sides

I want someone who makes me
laugh & who adores me
no matter how bad I get,
she said & I laughed.

What? she said, I'm just
trying to be honest.

>Requirements #1

I ask only 2 things, she said.
Tell me the truth
as soon as you know it.

What else? I said.

Tell me really romantic lies
the rest of the time, she said
& then she laughed

& I was forced to
grab her & tell her
something true
right then & there.

>Requirements #2

surprised she could hear a word
the way my heart jumped
up & down on the couch,
laughing & saying
whatever old thing
came into its head

> Babbling Heart

at first it sounded like she was anxious, but he
listened closely enough that finally he heard
her excitement about how closely he listened.

> Discerning Audience

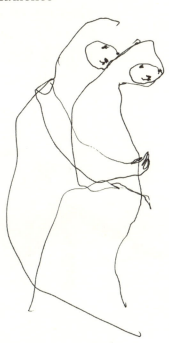

Today is a day
when I look out
over my life & I see
you there & I know
there is more reason
to this world than we
will ever understand.

> More Reason

She wrapped her heart carefully
with beautiful paper & ribbon
& her eyes sparkled
with the thought of
unwrapping it
together with me.

    Gift Heart

Once there was a boy & a girl, he said
& then he stopped & looked at her.
    OK, she said, what happened next?
        He stepped closer &
        kissed her on the nose.
        I think they wing it
        from there, he said.

        Open Plan

Sometimes,
I wake beside
you in the dark
& I feel you
there &

for a moment
there's only your
soft breathing,

& this life we've made together
with bodies & starlight & love.

This Life Together

filling places
he didn't
know were
empty until
he woke up
this morning
beside her

New Day

Low-key mainly
because she's got
enough going on
inside that she
doesn't need more
people around her
ready to freak out
at a moment's notice

Low Key

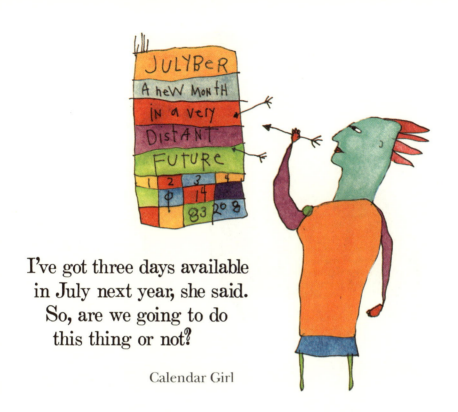

I've got three days available
in July next year, she said.
So, are we going to do
this thing or not?

Calendar Girl

even after
all these winters,
I see you sitting there,
perched at the edge of
sunlight, feeling like
the invitation of spring

Invitation of Spring

I usually only listen to talk radio in the car on the way to work, he said.

The kind of job I have, he added, it helps to be angry.

Talk Radio

How's the job hunt going? I said. She sighed. I can't help laughing when people do stupid things, she said, so basically I'm unemployable.

Skill Set

God invents musical theatre. Satan voluntarily opts for Hell.

Breaking Point

starting another morning in a straitjacket & I have to tell you spending the first couple of hours every day escaping gets old pretty fast

Escape Routine

Things I Know About Raising Children

(distilled into a few short lines because all we need is another expert who goes on & on, like every child out there isn't completely & utterly unique & frustrating all at the same time.)

1. Children want to know how things work, so they can play, too. (This actually goes for adults, too. But that's in another part of the book.)
2. Children see pretty clearly what we often forget. That the WORLD is AMAZING!
3. It takes a lot of work to convince a child that the world isn't amazing. So, here's a question for you: why on earth would you want to work at something like that? Oh, you mean you did it accidentally? Well, stop it. Go find other work you enjoy more. (That's better for you anyway...)
4. When they tell you what they want to do, listen to them. If it looks to you like it won't kill them, tell them to go do it. Because it might be the exact thing that lights them up. Even if it's not, it'll usually be pretty entertaining.

5. Let it slip now & then that you don't know everything. this will work in your favor when they get to be teenagers. & they say you don't know everything. you know. You can just smile & say THAT'S what I've been trying to tell you & they'll stop for a moment & then all of a sudden. they'll start giggling like they're 8 again & in that moment you'll know they're going to turn out fine (& you can relax, because that's all you were ever worried about in the first place. Right?)

First Law of Social Thermodynamics

No anxiety is ever lost. It is simply transferred to nearby people & objects until everyone is a little more nervous than usual.

                First Law

I think most of our anxiety comes from having to die before we figure it out, he said & then he shook his head.

I think the rest just comes from having to die.

       Sum Total

here's where I keep
   my biggest fears & you'll notice
there's not a whole lot of room
   for them to stretch

   because I'd rather have them
   stiff & grumpy & out of shape,
so when I let them out, they get tired
really quickly & just want to get
back to laying on the couch
   in the dark, mumbling
      to themselves.

        Fear Box

I'm really good at breaking down a problem into small enough parts that everything falls through the cracks

& voilá, problem solved.

Problem Solver

Things They Tell You Before You Were Born
(in case you were wondering why a lot of this stuff seems vaguely familiar)

1. Life will bump up against you & it'll be awhile before you stop taking it personally but the sooner you do that, the easier it gets

2. It's all about Love. Even the parts you decide are really hard.

3. You're not going to have to do this alone but you're going to take awhile to figure that out, too, especially if you end up in America.

Things They Don't Tell You Before You were Born (because, most likely, there are quotas & they don't want a lot of people backing out at the last minute)

1. Everything good we're telling you you're going to forget & you'll only start to remember once you give up acting like you know what you're doing. This can take a long time.

2. You're going to end up with people who do crazy stuff, but who act like it's normal & you, who just wants to have fun being alive, have to go along with it so they'll feed you. After a few years like this, you'll start doing the same crazy stuff. (Obviously, we're still working out some of the kinks.)

3. There'll be so much cool stuff to play with it'll take you awhile to settle down. There's a good chance we'll lose you along the way to some of those things. It's OK. You just die & then we'll tell you everything all over again & we'll all keep our fingers crossed & hope it goes better the next time.

I find myself
looking in the
mirror a lot &
asking myself
for advice, she said.
I figure someone
as old as me should
know something
by now.

Advice

I kept trying to be
what you wanted,
she said, but at a
certain point you
needed to stop
adding to the list.

Limits

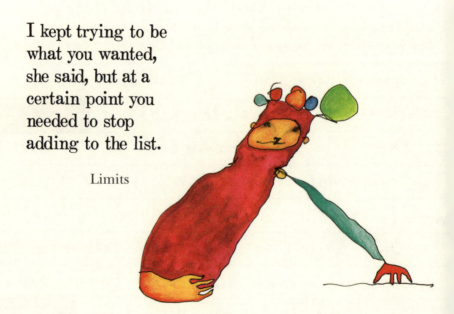

Today, I'm setting the bar really low,
he said, so there's nothing between me
& getting to bed early.

Setting The Bar

At that age where she's figured out
that living pretty much happens
no matter what you're doing, so it
might as well be fun.

Life Choice

My mind is
in a thousand
places at once,
except right here
where it could be
keeping me company
when I need it most.

Mind Game

finding loose
change & pieces
of himself once
he started
rearranging
everything in
here & he's been
amazed at how
often he says Oh,
that's where
that went.

Loose Change

Science vs religion, he said, who'd win?
Probably religion, I said.
OK, religion vs Chuck Norris? he said
& I laughed.

Never mind, he said.
Stupid question.

No Contest

no matter what someone says, she says Oh, I did that once, too, because she believes in reincarnation, so, most likely, she did

Life Experience

START A NEW RELIGION with COMMON HOUSEHOLD ITEMS

1. a potato stamp. Carve a cool symbol for your new religion out of a potato. You can stamp it pretty much on anything, even people's hands & foreheads (though it's probably best not to tell them it's for a new religion. I usually say it's free admission to Six Flags, or 10% off at Sam's Club & then they just let me stamp as much as I want.)

Also, if someone does figure it out & takes it from you & throws it on the ground & jumps up & down on it, you can just say, Ha-ha, there's plenty more where that came from & you can go make another one, in about 2 minutes.

Start a New Religion in Your Spare Time

Let's fall in love, he said & she said OK & he blinked. I didn't think it'd be that easy, he said & she patted his hand.

Love is not the hard part, she said. The hard part is trying not to freak out about what you've just done.

Hard Part

I like to live extravagantly in my mind, she said, but in real life I keep to the edges because I bruise easily.

Fringe Dweller

Prometheus

What are you doing? I said.
Learning to trust myself, she
said. It's easier if I just sit
here though, she added, so
I don't break anything.

Learning Curve

You are
a mystery,
I said & she
looked at me
for a moment
& then she sat
down & asked
me to tell her
more things
like that the
whole night.

Woman of Mystery

Suitably Ambiguous

What could go wrong? I said & she shook her head. I thought you had more imagination than that, she said.

Fertile Imagination

I've never been good with current events, she told us.

I always keep getting bogged down with simple things, like 'why are we here?'

Simple Things

started out as
a day trip, but
it turned out longer
because both of them
were too stubborn to
admit they were
tired of it.

Day Trip

Once there was
a girl who only
did things that
made her happy.

The only time she
wasn't happy was
when she forgot that
she only did things
that made her happy.

The End.

A VeRY SHoRT SToRY
with a very shoRt moRAL..

You're doing it wrong, she said & I said what part? You explaining it to me, she said & then she patted my arm as if that covered everything.

Constructive Criticism

Her big plan has her running the world in the end & the only thing in the way is all the billions of other people who have different plans

Big Plan

We're talking about feelings, she said, so there are no wrong answers

(but I had been around her enough to know that wasn't exactly true)

Wrong Answer

the irksome thing is that no matter how convincing she's been about the end of all joy, he decided to be happy, so she's found it's much easier to just pretend that he's dead

Playing Dead

I've always found that saying something true, she said, is a good way to start.

Well, he said, some cats are fat & she laughed.

Way to go for it, she said.

Open Communication

Fantasy Life

Questionable Value

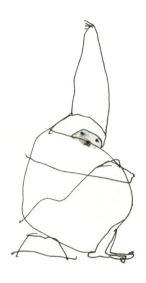

Today's the day
I have to be an
adult, he said &
she rolled her eyes.

Don't worry, she said,
wearing long pants for
a couple of hours doesn't
make you an adult
permanently.

Gradual Process

What makes you
an adult? he said
& I said it's mainly
a height requirement
& the willingness
to keep quiet
when people say
stupid things.

Adult Club

Now & then, I try to listen without knowing anything. It's a nice break from all the other days where I just talk without knowing anything.

              Nice Break

I know it's best not to be bitter about some of the people I've known, she said, but some days that takes a lot of ignoring the facts.

              Ignoring Facts

What is your intuition telling you? I said & she shook her head. My intuition is telling me to go back home & take a nap, she said.

              Sixth Sense

Dress Up Box

I always used to tell the truth, but people just thought I was being funny. So, I gave up & started lying & now I'm much more believable.

Credibility

What are your strengths? I said.

I don't suppose knowing when microwave popcorn is almost done is where you're going with this, he said.

Strong Sense

What do you have to say for yourself? she said & I asked if we could save some time & have her tell me the right answer.

Right Answer

Dramatic Flair

I'm disgusted with everyone but you, she said.

Why's that? I said.

Because you're right here, she said, & it wouldn't be polite.

Manners

particularly fond of giving advice for stuff he's only read about, because he's been too scared to go out & try it for himself.

Safety First

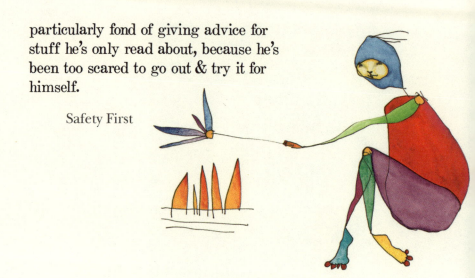

I'm too busy to breathe, she said. Breathe faster then, I said & she laughed for a surprisingly long time, considering she had no air.

Quick Breathing

I'm more a middle path sort of person, he said, as long it keeps going downhill.

Middle Path

I'm not here
to keep you
from the places
you feel you have
to go, she said.

When you're ready,
I'm here to remind
you of the way home.

The Way Home

certain of very few
things & despite what
you may think it makes
life pretty easy because
he's not so quick to mouth
off like everybody else
he knows.

An Uncertain Man

I know he's not really gone, she said, but
the world still feels smaller to me today.

                Smaller World

It is still so new & all
we see is the empty space,
but that is not how it is in
the landscape of the heart.
There, there is no empty
space & he still laughs &
grapples with ideas & plans
& nods wisely with
each of us in turn.

We are proud
to have known him.

We are proud to have
called him friend.

        Landscape of the
        Heart (for Erik)

I never knew emptiness could weigh
so much, she said. I can barely hold it.

  So I sat beside her & reached for
her hand & we held it, for as long
as it took, together.

      The Weight of Air

decided early on that she wanted
independence more than she
wanted love

    & it took her half her life
    to figure out she could
    have had both

        Deciding Bigger

I'm tired of hiding, I said
& she smiled.

That's good, she said,
because I'm tired of
pretending it doesn't hurt.

        Hiding Game

filled with thoughts of loveliness & enough chocolate so that any of the non-lovely thoughts basically get drowned at birth

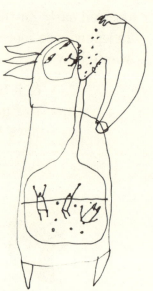

WHAT I KNOW ABOUT CHANGE ⇒ THIS is why we have feet & minds — because if we don't like something we can walk away or think some different thoughts. just like that.

sorting out things based on a strange combination of stuff he's read about in books & things he's tried out once or twice in his head

(so there's always a chance it'll fall apart in a spectacular fashion)

Inexact Science

Nothing moved except a patch of sunlight across the floor.

I confused safety for love again, she said. I nodded.

I wish you hadn't been confused, too, she said.

Mistaken Identity

I know this is all about me, she said, but could you at least pretend, so we could share the blame for a while?

My life would be
fine, she said, if
they'd all stop
judging me.
She paused for
a moment.
& if I stopped
agreeing with
them, she added.

Agreeable

likes to think of it
as multi-tasking, but
really, it's doing a bunch
of stuff poorly enough that
someone else feels compelled
to step in & save her

Scatter Tasking

Of course I already know the best thing to do, but it'll have to wait a little while longer. I'm still convinced I can get my own way.

Best Thing

Things to Know about THE FUTURE ooo

the main thing to know about the future is that it's only good for one thing: it keeps us being all anxious, which is probably exactly what we need to get stuff done

. The future doesn't have to look any particular way. but around here, if it doesn't, a lot of people will never speak to you again.

. The future is a guess. Sometimes you guess right. Be careful with that, because pretty soon you'll be guessing all the time & acting like it's true & next thing you know you'll forget you do your best work in the present.

Things to Know About the Future

deciding today that
reality is easier if you can
put it in a box & ignore
that it keeps slipping out
& messing everything up.

Reality Box

hoping the end
is near, mainly
because he's already
seen the beginning &
the middle & now he's
up for something new

The End Is Near

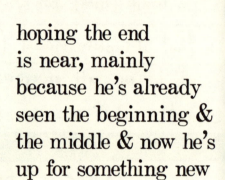

I don't think of it as
avoiding, he said. I
think of it as
another opportunity
to practice ignoring
things that bug me.

Steady Practice

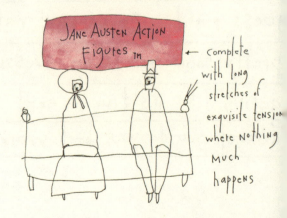

I'm here to build the future, he
said & she looked up & said
How about we start you on the
present then? & he was fine
with that as long as there was
a chance to move up

& years later, he finally
understood why she smiled &
let him jump right in.

Begin Here

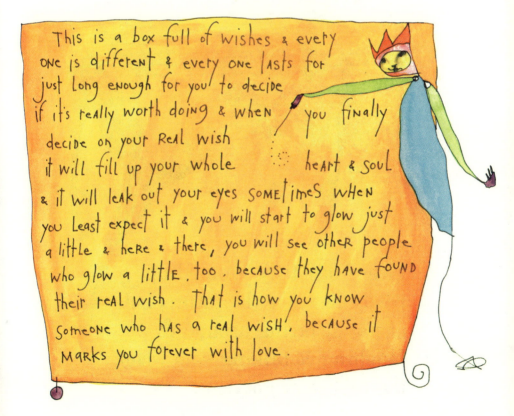

Box Full of Wishes (Sophie's Choice)

Every day they jumped up ready to make the future, but at night, laying around & laughing & talking was when the real work got done.

Real Work

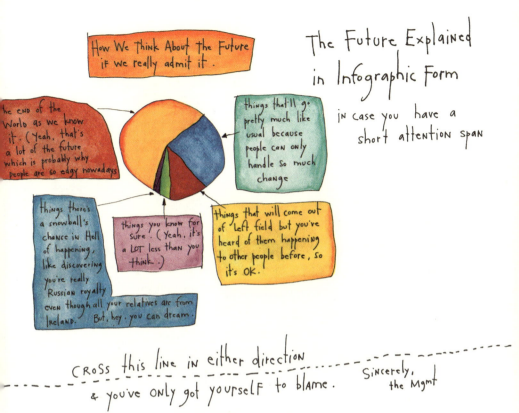

The Future Explained

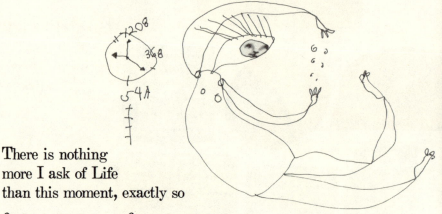

There is nothing
more I ask of Life
than this moment, exactly so

& she looked at me & my heart danced
like a candle flame from her breath on my chest

    & forever suddenly seemed
      like too short a time

          This Exact Moment

You have so many
perfect days, he said
& she smiled & said
it's a lot easier when
you expect them
to be perfect,
no matter
how they
go.

Perfect Days

How do you know? she said & the answers fell like feathers,

or the first snowflakes of November, light & without words.

I looked in her eyes & smiled.

You just know, I said.

Intuition

It is not what you first think.
There is no effort of will,
no firm resolve in the face
of this thing called living.

There is only paying attention
to the quiet each morning,
while you hold your cup
in the cool air

& then
that moment
you choose
to spread your
love like a cloth
upon the table &
invite the whole day
in again.

Invitation

Rules for making the world:

1. Stand up & do the thing you see needs doing.
2. That's it.
   (If it was easy, we'd be having a different conversation.)

   Action Plan

I still see clearly that moment when she held my face in her hands, her voice low & fierce. Just because you don't remember what you came to do, she said, doesn't mean you didn't do it

& now, I think of those words each morning & I give a prayer of thanks for all of our lives

& offer my heart again to the day.

   Offering

I remember the morning we walked through the city together. You know, she said, leaning into me, there's only love & what you do with it.

& suddenly, like the first scent of green things at the end of winter, it was all around me & everywhere there were people with eyes shining & it was so clear they had been there all along that I had to laugh

& wonder how I ever thought we could fail.

Only Love

About the Artist

To tell the truth, I have no idea what would be useful to know about me. The fact that I like to tease cats publicly, even though, privately, I think they're fabulous? Or that one of the things that settles me into the world is the feel of a warm mug of tea in my hands as I look out at the garden? Or that I love summer lightning storms & the sound of rain on a metal roof?

Maybe this is more like it: I'm the father of two boys who, in the blink of these last six years, turned into extraordinary young men, artists in their own right. Since they were homeschooled, I've had the luxury of being around their wildly creative minds for years. You'll often see them showing up in the stories.

I came to making art & stories almost by accident. I've been a playwright, waiter, tennis player, chef, contract archaeologist, accountant, systems architect & computer programmer, among other things. Along the way, I figured out that I actually liked making up stories more than almost anything else & I haven't stopped since.

What else? I've collected a couple of degrees over the years. I graduated from Luther College in Decorah, Iowa with a BA in various things & I've got an MFA in Fibre & Mixed Media (in case you think I'm just one of those popular artists who can't cut it in the real world of academia) from JFK University in Orinda, California.

This is my ninth, tenth, or eleventh book, depending on what you count. I hope you'll think of it an invitation to the conversation that weaves through all the earlier books, a conversation filled with imagination & connection & play. Pull up a comfy chair & join in. I'm glad you're here...

About StoryPeople

StoryPeople has come to mean many things. StoryPeople can be the wood sculptures created by Brian Andreas. They can be one of the hundreds of his colorful story prints. They're the community of people on the web site who share their own stories as they make sense of the world we're making together & they're any of the hundreds of thousands of people worldwide who have come to know & love his work.

StoryPeople is also the name we give to the company of friends & co-workers who make it all possible. From our small town in Iowa, we distribute Brian Andreas' stories to galleries & bookstores all over the planet. We play with the web, imagining, almost daily, new ways to bring the stories to more people. We believe in the power of stories to transform our world & we believe now is the time, more than ever before. Our business is to give our world & ourselves tools to imagine & create & heal. Stories that cherish the quiet moments. Stories of a world that works for everyone. Stories about a world worth saving.

The sculptures, the prints & the books are available in galleries, gift stores & bookstores throughout the US, Canada & the EU (along with a few others scattered about the world) & on our web site. Please feel free to call, or write, for more information, or drop in on the web at **www.storypeople.com**

StoryPeople
P.O. Box 7
Decorah, IA 52101
USA

800.476.7178
563.382.8060
563.382.0263 FAX

orders@storypeople.com